OF LISIEUX

꙳

MEDITATIONS WITH
THE LITTLE FLOWER

Joseph D. White, Ph.D.

QUOTES BY ST. THÉRÈSE TRANSLATED FROM
THE ORIGINAL FRENCH BY TERESA HAWES

Our Sunday Visitor Publishing Division
Our Sunday Visitor, Inc.
Huntington, Indiana 46750

Copyright © 2013 by Joseph D. White. Published 2013.

18 17 16 15 14 13   1 2 3 4 5 6 7 8 9

ISBN: 978-1-61278-591-2 (Inventory No. T1287)
eISBN: 978-1-61278-348-2
LCCN: 2013947136

Cover design: Rebecca J. Heaston
Cover photo: The Crosiers
Interior design: Dianne Nelson

PRINTED IN THE UNITED STATES OF AMERICA

CONTENTS

INTRODUCTION

ST. THÉRÈSE OF LISIEUX, born Marie-Françoise-Thérèse Martin, lived in France from 1873 to 1897. Her short life was marked by suffering, first in the loss of her mother at age four, then in separation from her older sisters, who joined the convent before Thérèse was old enough to follow, and later by her own slow death of tuberculosis. Despite all the hardships of her twenty-four years, Thérèse was, by all accounts, a joyful, peaceful soul.

Thérèse wrote her memoirs at the command of her sister, who was her mother superior at the time. She scoffed at the idea that anyone would actually be interested in reading about her life, but her writings quickly circulated around the world. Here was a very ordinary person who had found an extraordinary spirituality in everyday life. Hers was a spirituality of offering even the most mundane tasks to God, and performing them as if working for Christ himself. This was not a new idea, as St. Paul says in Colossians 3:23: "Whatever your task, work heartily, as serving the Lord and not men." Still, Thérèse's straightforward way of applying this principle to her own life served as an inspiration for countless faithful, including the likes of Blessed Mother Teresa of Calcutta and St. Josemaría Escrivá.

In assembling this collection, it struck me anew how closely many of Thérèse's words echo the words of Sacred Scripture. She obviously knew the Scriptures well and found simple, yet profound ways to apply the Word of God to her own daily life. In his second letter to the Corinthians, St. Paul writes that "you show that you are a letter from Christ delivered by us, written not with ink but with the Spirit of the living God, not on tablets of stone but on tablets of human hearts" (3:3).

The life of St. Thérèse embodies these words. She was truly a living letter from Christ. As we listen to God with our sister Thérèse, may we, too, be inspired to do "small things with great love."

– JOSEPH D. WHITE, PH.D.
Feast Day of St. Thérèse of Lisieux
October 1, 2012

NOTE REGARDING
THE TRANSLATION

THE SOURCE OF THE QUOTATIONS OF ST. THÉRÈSE that was used in this book was Thérèse's *Complete Works*, published by Editions du Cerf/ Desclée de Brouwer:

> *Sainte Thérèse de l'Enfant-Jésus et de la Sainte-Face*: *Œuvres Complètes* (Textes et Dernières Paroles). Paris: Editions du Cerf/Desclée de Brouwer, 1992.

St. Thérèse's autobiography, *Story of a Soul*, is in fact composed of three distinct manuscripts written at different times to three different people. They are referred to as Manuscript A, Manuscript B, and Manuscript C. The page numbers of these manuscripts are determined per sheet of paper. In other words, page 1 has a front side (recto) and a back side (verso). So, **Ms. A 2v** means that the text may be found in Manuscript A, on the back of page 2.

In parentheses, after each citation, is the page of the *Complete Works* where the quotation may be found. So **(OC, p. 72)** means *Œuvres Complètes*, page 72. **Ms. A69v-A70r** means that the passage begins on the back of page 69 and continues to the front of page 70 in Manuscript A.

Meditation 36 (page 48), for example, uses the numbering of Thérèse's written prayers established by Bishop Guy Gaucher and his team as they were elaborating the critical edition. Some quotes are from Thérèse's letters. **LT** is simply the abbreviation for them. The numbering follows the critical edition. Some quotes are from *Last Conversations*. These are identified by dates, then in the order in which they were written down. So **July 13, 15** means that on July 13, this is the fifteenth notation of things Thérèse said that day.

– TERESA HAWES, TRANSLATOR

MEDITATIONS WITH
THE LITTLE FLOWER

1.
GOD'S LOVE REVEALED IN HUMANITY

Our Lord's love is revealed just as well through
a simple soul totally surrendered to His grace
as through one much more richly endowed.
– Ms. A 2v (OC, p. 72)

༚

For God shows no partiality.
– ROMANS 2:11

2.
GROWTH THROUGH TRIAL

I have reached a point in my life where I
can look back over the past; my soul has
matured in the crucible of suffering
from both within and without.
– Ms. A 3R (OC, P. 73)

❧

Count it all joy, my brethren, when you meet
various trials, for you know that the testing
of your faith produces steadfastness. And let
steadfastness have its full effect, that you may
be perfect and complete, lacking in nothing.
– JAMES 1:2-4

3.
GIFTEDNESS

It seems to me that if a little flower could
speak, it would simply say what the Good Lord
has done for it, without trying to hide His gifts.
It would not, motivated by false humility,
claim to be plain or without fragrance, nor
would it say the sun had faded its colors
or storms had broken its stem, knowing
full well the opposite was true.
– Ms. A 3v (OC, PP. 73-74)

࿇

"You are the light of the world. A city set on a
hill cannot be hid. Nor do men light a lamp and
put it under a bushel, but on a stand, and
it gives light to all in the house. Let your
light so shine before men, that they may see
your good works and give glory to your
Father who is in heaven."
– MATTHEW 5:14-16

4.
SELF-DENIAL

Later on, when perfection became my goal, I understood that to become a saint you need to suffer a great deal, [and to] always make the most perfect choice and forget about yourself.
– MS. A 10R (OC, P. 84)

☙

And he said to all, "If any man would come after me, let him deny himself and take up his cross daily and follow me."
– LUKE 9:23

5.
POWER OVER EVIL

A soul in the state of grace has nothing
to fear from demons; they are cowards,
frightened away by a child's gaze.
– Ms. A 10v (OC, p. 85)

⤙

Little children, you are of God, and have
overcome them; for he who is in you is
greater than he who is in the world.
– 1 JOHN 4:4

6.
HEAVENLY JOY

I understood we would
experience perfect joy only in Heaven.
– Ms. A 14v (OC, P. 92)

❧

"He will wipe away every tear from their eyes,
and death shall be no more, neither shall
there be mourning nor crying nor pain any
more, for the former things have passed away."
– REVELATION 21:4

7.
CONQUERING FEARS

I consider your[1] having made me get over
my fears as a true grace.
– Ms. A 18v (OC, p. 98)

࿔

"Fear not, little flock, for it is your Father's good
pleasure to give you the kingdom."
– LUKE 12:32

---

[1] Ms. A was written to Thérèse's blood sister Pauline,
Mother Agnes (also known as Sister Agnes of Jesus), who
was also prioress at the time. After their mother's death,
when Thérèse was four, Pauline became Thérèse's "second
mother." The reference here is to Thérèse's childhood fear
of the dark.

8.
STRENGTH TO ENDURE TRIALS

How good the Good Lord is! He does indeed
give us trials and the strength to get through
them in equal measure.
– MS. A 21R (OC, P. 102)

৵

God is faithful, and he will not let you be
tempted beyond your strength, but with the
temptation will also provide the way of escape,
that you may be able to endure it.
– 1 CORINTHIANS 10:13

9.
PERSEVERANCE

I contemplated that luminous furrow for a long time.[2] It was an image of grace pointing out the way the little white-sailed boat[3] was to go. At Pauline's side, I resolved never to take my soul away from Jesus' gaze so it might sail peacefully toward the Homeland of Heaven.

– Ms. A 22R (OC, P. 103)

❧

Therefore, since we are surrounded by so great a cloud of witnesses, let us also lay aside every weight, and sin which clings so closely, and let us run with perseverance the race that is set before us, looking to Jesus the pioneer and perfecter of our faith, who for the joy that was set before him endured the cross, despising the shame, and is seated at the right hand of the throne of God.

– HEBREWS 12:1-2

---

[2] In August 1878, when Thérèse was five, she watched the sun setting on the ocean for the first time.

[3] Thérèse often used a little boat as an image of her own soul.

10.
TRUE GLORY

But soon the Good Lord made me sense that
true glory is the one that lasts forever, and
to attain it there is no need to accomplish
remarkable exploits.[4] Instead, you need to hide
[your good works] such that your left hand
knows not what the right one is doing.
– Ms. A 31v-32r (OC, P. 119)

༈

"But when you give alms, do not let your left
hand know what your right hand is doing,
so that your alms may be in secret; and your
Father who sees in secret will reward you."
– MATTHEW 6:3-4

---

[4] Thérèse used to enjoy reading adventure stories about
knights in shining armor.

11.
JUSTIFICATION THROUGH CHRIST

He Himself, content with my feeble efforts,
will lift me up and, sharing His infinite
merits with me, make me a saint.
– Ms. A 32R (OC, P. 120)

❧

For as many of you as were baptized into
Christ have put on Christ.
– GALATIANS 3:27

12.
MATERIALISM

Our Alençon friends were too worldly; they
knew too well how to enjoy earthly pleasures
while serving the Good Lord. They did not
meditate often enough on death.
– Ms. A 32v (OC, P. 120)

❧

"Sell your possessions, and give alms; provide
yourselves with purses that do not grow old,
with a treasure in the heavens that does not
fail, where no thief approaches and no moth
destroys. For where your treasure is, there will
your heart be also. Let your loins be girded and
your lamps burning, and be like men who are
waiting for their master to come home from the
marriage feast, so that they may open to him at
once when he comes and knocks."
– LUKE 12:33-36

13.
SELF-ABANDONMENT

Thérèse had disappeared just like a drop of
water into the depths of the ocean; Jesus alone
remained: her Master, her King.[5]
– Ms. A 35R (OC, P. 125)

❧

"He must increase, but I must decrease."
– JOHN 3:30

---

[5] This is part of Thérèse's description of her First Communion.

14.
LASTING JOY

The most gorgeous days are followed by
darkness; only on the day of the First, the one
and only, the eternal Communion, in Heaven,
will the sun never set!
– Ms. A 35V-36R (OC, P. 126)

∽

Your sun shall no more go down,
nor your moon withdraw itself;
for the LORD will be your everlasting light,
and your days of mourning shall be ended.
– ISAIAH 60:20

15.
EARTHLY ATTACHMENTS

How can a heart given over to earthly
affections be intimately united to God?
I can tell that is impossible.
– Ms. A 38r (OC, p. 130)

෨

"He who loves father or mother more than me
is not worthy of me; and he who loves son or
daughter more than me is not worthy of me."
– MATTHEW 10:37

16.
RELIANCE ON GOD

The Good Lord has given me the grace never to
be discouraged by anything that will not last.
– Ms. A 43R (OC, P. 139)

I know how to be abased, and I know how
to abound; in any and all circumstances I
have learned the secret of facing plenty and
hunger, abundance and want. I can do all
things in him who strengthens me.
– PHILIPPIANS 4:12-13

17.
CHANGE OF HEART

When I remember the past, my soul overflows
with gratitude, seeing the favors I have received
from Heaven; there has been such a change in
me that I am unrecognizable.
– MS. 43R (OC, P. 139)

~

Therefore, if any one is in Christ, he is a new
creation; the old has passed away, behold,
the new has come. All this is from God, who
through Christ reconciled us to himself and
gave us the ministry of reconciliation.
– 2 CORINTHIANS 5:17-18

18.
STRENGTH FOR BATTLE

Jesus, the sweet Infant only an hour old,
changed the night of my soul into torrents
of light. On that night when He took on
weakness and suffering for my sake, He
made me strong and brave. He armed me
with His weapons, and ever since that
blessed night I have never been defeated in
any battle. On the contrary, I have gone
from one victory to the next, and thus began,
so to speak, to run as fast as a giant!
– Ms. A 44v (OC, P. 141)

❧

"For thou didst gird me with strength
for the battle; thou didst make my
assailants sink under me."
– 2 SAMUEL 22:40

19.
LIVING TEMPLES

He does not come down from Heaven each
day to stay in the gold ciborium. He comes
down to find another Heaven He cherishes
infinitely more than the first, the Heaven
of our souls, made in His image, living
temples of the Most Blessed Trinity!
– Ms. A 48v (OC, P. 148)

≈

Examine yourselves, to see whether you are
holding to your faith. Test yourselves. Do you
not realize that Jesus Christ is in you?
– 2 CORINTHIANS 13:5

20.
MATURITY

Whenever a gardener takes great care of a piece
of fruit he wants to have ripened ahead of time,
it is never to leave it hanging on the tree, but to
display it on a beautifully decorated table.
– Ms. A 48v (OC, P. 149)

❧

And I am sure that he who began a good
work in you will bring it to completion
at the day of Jesus Christ.
– PHILIPPIANS 1:6

21.
SPIRITUAL DIRECTION

So many more souls would become holy if they
had good spiritual directors!
– Ms. A 53R (OC, P. 157)

&

The aim of our charge is love that issues from a
pure heart and a good conscience and sincere
faith. Certain persons by swerving from these
have wandered away into vain discussion,
desiring to be teachers of the law, without
understanding either what they are saying or
the things about which they make assertions.
– 1 TIMOTHY 1:5-7

22.
THE PURE OF HEART

An uncomplicated, upright soul sees no evil
anywhere since evil does indeed exist only in
impure hearts, and not in material objects.
– Ms. A 57R (OC, P. 165)

๛

To the pure all things are pure, but to the
corrupt and unbelieving nothing is pure; their
very minds and consciences are corrupted.
– TITUS 1:15

23.
FOCUSING ON ETERNAL THINGS

I will easily forget my own little vantage point
when I see God's greatness and power. I want
to love Him and Him alone. I won't be so
unfortunate as to get attached to insignificant
things, now that my heart has sensed what
Jesus has in store "for those who love Him"!
– MS. A 58R (OC, P. 167)

☙

Set your minds on things that are above,
not on things that are on earth.
– COLOSSIANS 3:2

24.
THE MYSTERY OF HEAVEN

So what will it be like when we receive
Communion in the King of Heaven's
eternal dwelling place?
– Ms. A 60R (OC, P. 170)

∾

"What no eye has seen, nor ear heard,
nor the heart of man conceived,
what God has prepared for those who love him."
– 1 CORINTHIANS 2:9

25.
SEEING GOD AS HE IS

What He has in store for us is His glorious
palace, where we will no longer see Him
hidden under the appearance of a child or
a white host, but exactly as He is, in the
radiance of His infinite splendor!

– Ms. A 60R (OC, P. 170)

☙

Beloved, we are God's children now; it does
not yet appear what we shall be, but we know
that when he appears we shall be like him,
for we shall see him as he is.

– 1 JOHN 3:2

26.
LASTING JOY

I know well that joy cannot be found in
the things around us; it is found in the
innermost depths of the soul.
– Ms. A 65R (OC, P. 179)

"Do not lay up for yourselves treasures on
earth, where moth and rust consume and
where thieves break in and steal, but lay up
for yourselves treasures in heaven, where
neither moth nor rust consumes and where
thieves do not break in and steal."
– MATTHEW 6:19-20

27.
REJOICING IN SUFFERING

Jesus made me understand that He wanted
to give me souls through the cross, and my
attraction for suffering grew at the same pace
as my suffering increased.
– Ms. A 69v (OC, P. 187)

❧

Now I rejoice in my sufferings for your sake,
and in my flesh I complete what is lacking
in Christ's afflictions for the sake of his
body, that is, the church.
– COLOSSIANS 1:24

28.
DETACHMENT FROM
WORLDLY STATUS

He whose kingdom is not of this world showed
me that true wisdom consists in "wanting to
be ignored and counted as nothing."[6]
– Ms. A 71R (OC, P. 189)

৵

"My kingship is not of this world; if my
kingship were of this world, my servants would
fight, that I might not be handed over to the
Jews; but my kingship is not from the world."
– JOHN 18:36

---

[6] OC, p. 1267, footnote 323, indicates that this is a quote
from *The Imitation of Christ* (which Thérèse knew practi-
cally by heart).

29.
GOD GIVES US THE DESIRES
OF OUR HEARTS

How merciful is the way by which the Good
Lord has always led me; never has He made me
long for anything without giving it to me.
– MS. A 71R (OC, P. 190)

꙾

Take delight in the LORD,
and he will give you the desires of your heart.
– PSALM 37:4

30.
CHOOSING GOD'S WILL

Since I had given myself to Jesus to please and console Him, it was not mine to make Him do my will instead of His.

– Ms. A 73V-74R (OC, P. 194)

❧

And he said, "Abba, Father, all things are possible to thee; remove this cup from me; yet not what I will, but what thou wilt."

– MARK 14:36

31.
ACCEPTING OUR IMPERFECTION

I quickly realized that the farther along you
are on this path, the farther away from your
destination you think you are, so now I am
resigned to seeing myself still imperfect,
and that is my source of joy.
– Ms. A 74R (OC, PP. 194-195)

∽

I will all the more gladly boast of my
weaknesses, that the power of Christ
may rest upon me.
– 2 CORINTHIANS 12:9

32.
True Poverty

Poverty consists in letting yourself be deprived
not only of things you like but even more of
those [things] that seem indispensable.
– Ms. A 74R-74V (OC, P. 195)

❧

"No one can serve two masters; for either he
will hate the one and love the other, or he will
be devoted to the one and despise the other.
You cannot serve God and mammon."
– Matthew 6:24

33.
SLEEPING IN GOD'S PRESENCE

I should be distressed about sleeping
(for seven years) during my times of silent
prayer and thanksgiving; well, I am not.
I think that parents love their little children
just as much when they are asleep as when
they are awake; I think that in order to perform
surgery, doctors put their patients to sleep.
– Ms. A 75v-76r (OC, p. 197)

༈

In peace I will both lie down and sleep;
for thou alone, O LORD, makest me
dwell in safety.
– PSALM 4:8

34.
DEPENDING ON GOD
TO MEET OUR NEEDS

Jesus does not want to give me supplies
to store away; He constantly nourishes
me with food that is ever new.
– Ms. A 76R (OC, P. 198)

❧

"Give us this day our daily bread."
– MATTHEW 6:11

35.
AVOIDING THE STAIN OF SIN

O Jesus, my divine spouse, may I never lose
my second baptismal garment;[7] take me away
before I commit the least little voluntary sin.
— PRAYER 2 (OC, P. 957)

Religion that is pure and undefiled before God
and the Father is this: to visit orphans and
widows in their affliction, and to keep oneself
unstained from the world.
— JAMES 1:27

---

[7] Theologians tell us that the self-giving through consecra-
tion by vows gives a grace akin to Baptism.

36.
LOVE

Jesus, I ask You only for peace and also love,
infinite love whose only limit is You, love that is
no longer me but You, my Jesus.
– PRAYER 2 (OC, P. 957)

᷿

And above all these put on love, which binds
everything together in perfect harmony.
– COLOSSIANS 3:14

37.
GOD'S MERCY AND TENDERNESS

In the depths of my heart, I knew it was true
that God might not be hurt by our involuntary
faults, for the Good Lord is more tender than
a Mother; well then, dear Mother,[8] are you not
always ready to forgive me for the little hurtful
actions I inflict on you involuntarily?
– Ms. A 80v (OC, p. 206)

&

The LORD is merciful and gracious,
slow to anger and abounding in steadfast love.
– PSALM 103:8

---

[8] This is addressed to Pauline, Mother Agnes, who, as
Thérèse said, was twice her mother (see footnote 1, p. 19).

38.
FEAR VS. LOVE

My nature is such that fear makes me
lose ground, while with love, not only
do I gain ground, I fly.
– Ms. A 80v (OC, P. 206)

৯

There is no fear in love, but perfect love
casts out fear.
– 1 JOHN 4:18

39.
GOD'S PLEASURE IN GIVING TO US

I surrendered to Jesus, not in order to receive
His visit[9] for my own consolation, but on the
contrary, for the joy of Him who is giving
Himself to me.
– Ms. A. 79v (OC, p. 204)

֍

"Fear not, little flock, for it is your Father's good
pleasure to give you the kingdom."
– LUKE 12:32

---

9 The context here is a thanksgiving prayer after
Communion.

40.
GOD'S POWER MADE PERFECT
IN WEAKNESS

I am far from being led by the way of fear;
I always know how to find the means to be
happy and take advantage of my miseries.
Doubtless, Jesus doesn't mind, for He seems to
encourage me along this path.
– MS. A 80R (OC, P. 205)

❧

But he said to me, "My grace is sufficient for
you, for my power is made perfect in weakness."
– 2 CORINTHIANS 12:9

41.
LOVE IS ESSENTIAL

I understand that without love, anything we
may do, however striking, is nothing.
– Ms. A 81v (OC, P. 207)

❧

If I speak in the tongues of men and of
angels, but have not love, I am a noisy gong
or a clanging cymbal. And if I have prophetic
powers, and understand all mysteries
and all knowledge, and if I have all faith,
so as to remove mountains, but have not love,
I am nothing. If I give away all I have, and if
I deliver my body to be burned, but have not
love, I gain nothing.
– 1 CORINTHIANS 13:1-3

42.
GOD ALONE SATISFIES

He alone is unchanging; He alone can
fulfill my immense desires.
– Ms. A 81v (OC, P. 207)

 ॐ

And my God will supply every need of yours
according to his riches in glory in Christ Jesus.
– PHILIPPIANS 4:19

43.
SACRIFICE

Here and now, in this life, in the smallest as
well as the biggest things, the God Lord gives a
hundredfold to the souls who have
left everything for His love.[10]
– Ms. A 81v (OC, P. 208)

❧

Jesus said, "Truly, I say to you, there is no one
who has left house or brothers or sisters or
mother or father or children or lands, for my
sake and for the gospel, who will not receive
a hundredfold now in this time, houses and
brothers and sisters and mothers and
children and lands, with persecutions,
and in the age to come eternal life."
– MARK 10:29-30

---

[10] The expected translation might be "out of love for Him,"
but given her teaching that we can truly love only with the
love He gives us, I stand by this. — Teresa Hawes

44.
FOLLOWING GOD'S WILL

Now surrender alone is my guide; I have no
other compass. I can no longer urgently ask for
anything except the perfect fulfillment of the
Good Lord's will in my soul.
– Ms. A 83R (OC, P. 210)

❧

And the world passes away, and the lust of it;
but he who does the will of God
abides for ever.
– 1 JOHN 2:17

45.
THE POWER OF LOVE

How sweet is the way of love! Doubtless you
may fall, you may be unfaithful, but Love,
knowing how to take advantage of everything,
has in no time burned up whatever makes
Jesus unhappy, leaving nothing but humble,
profound peace deep in your heart.
– Ms. A 83R (OC, P. 210)

⤜

Love bears all things, believes all things,
hopes all things, endures all things.
– 1 CORINTHIANS 13:7

46.
GOD'S INDWELLING

Never have I heard Him speak, but I can tell
He is present within me; He is constantly
guiding me, letting me know what I should
say or do. Just when I need it, I discover
light I had not yet seen.
– Ms. A 83v (OC, P. 211)

৵

Do you not know that you are God's temple
and that God's Spirit dwells in you?
– 1 CORINTHIANS 3:16

47.
BECKONED BY GOD'S KINDNESS

It seems to me that if everyone received the
same graces I do, nobody would be afraid of the
Good Lord; instead, He would be loved
to the utmost extreme. Out of love, without
any trembling, no soul would ever agree
to make Him unhappy.
– Ms. A 83v (OC, P. 211)

∂

Or do you presume upon the riches of his
kindness and forbearance and patience?
Do you not know that God's kindness is
meant to lead you to repentance?
– ROMANS 2:4

48.
GOD'S INFINITE MERCY

To me He has given His infinite Mercy;
through it I contemplate and adore all the
other divine perfections. So to me they
all seem to shine with love.
– Ms. A 83v (OC, p. 211)

❧

But God, who is rich in mercy, out of the great
love with which he loved us, even when we
were dead through our trespasses, made us
alive together with Christ (by grace you have
been saved), and raised us up with him, and
made us sit with him in the heavenly places in
Christ Jesus, that in the coming ages he might
show the immeasurable riches of his grace in
kindness toward us in Christ Jesus.
– EPHESIANS 2:4-7

49.
GOD'S UNDERSTANDING OF US

What sweet joy comes from the thought that
the Lord is just; in other words, that He
takes our weaknesses into account, that
He knows perfectly well how fragile our
nature is. What then could I fear?
– Ms. A 83v (OC, p. 211)

೪

For he knows our frame;
he remembers that we are dust.
– PSALM 103:14

50.
GOD'S JUSTICE

The infinitely just God who stooped down
with such goodness to forgive all the
prodigal son's sins, must He not also be
just to me who "am always with Him"?
– Ms. A 83v-84r (OC, pp. 211-212)

֍

"And he said to him, 'Son, you are always
with me, and all that is mine is yours.'"
– Luke 15:31

51.
ALL GOOD COMES FROM GOD

I need fear nothing from that now; on the
contrary, I can enjoy it, thanking the Good
Lord for whatever good He has graciously
decided to entrust to me.
– Ms. C 2R (OC, PP. 236-237)

⮞

Every good endowment and every perfect
gift is from above, coming down from the
Father of lights with whom there is no
variation or shadow due to change.
– JAMES 1:17

52.
GOD'S GRACE TO THE HUMBLE

As for me, I, too, would like to find an
elevator to lift me up to Jesus, for I am too little
to climb the steep staircase of perfection.
– Ms. C 3R (OC, P. 237)

～

But he gives more grace; therefore it says,
"God opposes the proud, but gives
grace to the humble."
– JAMES 4:6

53.
BECOMING LESS

Your arms, O Jesus, are the elevator that will lift
me up to Heaven. For that to happen, I don't
need to grow; on the contrary, I need to remain
little, and become so more and more.
– Ms. C 3R (OC, P. 238)

৯

"Truly, I say to you, whoever does not
receive the kingdom of God like a child
shall not enter it."
– MARK 10:15

54.
GOD'S POWER BEYOND OUR IMAGINATION

You know, my Mother, how rare are the souls
who do not measure divine power according
to their own narrow views.
– Ms. C 4R (OC, P. 239)

Now to him who by the power at work
within us is able to do far more abundantly
than all that we ask or think, to him be glory
in the church and in Christ Jesus to
all generations, for ever and ever. Amen.
– EPHESIANS 3:20-21

55.
GOOD FROM SUFFERING

If it were possible for You not to know about my suffering,[11] I would still be happy to endure it if in that way I could hinder or do penance for a single fault committed against the Faith.
– Ms. C 7R (OC, P. 243)

❧

So I ask you not to lose heart over what I am suffering for you, which is your glory.
– EPHESIANS 3:13

---

[11] Thérèse is speaking to God.

56.
WORKING FOR GOD'S GLORY

Often it is enough for the Lord that we
want to work for His glory.
– Ms. C 8v (OC, P. 245)

❧

So, whether you eat or drink,
or whatever you do, do all
to the glory of God.
– 1 CORINTHIANS 10:31

57.
LOVE IN THE HEARTS OF BELIEVERS

When our hearts are given to God, they
do not lose their natural tenderness;
on the contrary, this tenderness
increases, becoming purer
and more divine.
– Ms. C 9R (OC, PP. 245-246)

৵

"By this all men will know that you are my
disciples, if you have love for one another."
– JOHN 13:35

58.
BEARING OTHERS' BURDENS

Ah! Now I understand that perfect fraternal
charity consists in bearing with others'
faults, being not at all surprised at their
weaknesses, being edified by the smallest
virtuous acts we see them accomplish.
– Ms. C 12R (OC, P. 250)

ༀ

Bear one another's burdens, and
so fulfill the law of Christ.
– GALATIANS 6:2

59.
CHARITY

But I especially understand that charity is not
meant to stay locked up within our hearts.
– Ms. C 12R (OC, P. 250)

๛

Little children, let us not love in word
or speech but in deed and in truth.
– 1 JOHN 3:18

60.
ALL THINGS ARE POSSIBLE WITH GOD

Ah, Lord, I know You never command us
to do anything impossible.
– Ms. C 12v (OC, P. 250)

❧

I can do all things in him
who strengthens me.
– PHILIPPIANS 4:13

61.
THE POOR IN SPIRIT

Ah! What peace inundates the soul when it
raises itself above natural feelings! No, there is
no joy comparable to what someone who
is truly poor in spirit experiences.
– Ms. C 16v (OC, p. 256)

❧

"Blessed are the poor in spirit, for theirs
is the kingdom of heaven."
– MATTHEW 5:3

62.
GIVING TO OTHERS

So it is not enough to give to whomever asks
me for something; I need to foresee the desire,
seem very privileged and honored to lend a
hand, and if someone takes something I use, I
mustn't seem to wish I had it back but, on the
contrary, seem happy to be rid of it.
– Ms. C 16V-17R (OC, PP. 256-257)

❧

"… and from him who takes away your coat do
not withhold even your shirt. Give to every one
who begs from you; and of him who takes away
your goods do not ask them again."
– LUKE 6:29-30

63.
GRACE

Ah! What Jesus teaches is indeed the opposite
of our natural inclinations; without the help of
His grace, it would be impossible not only to
put it into practice but even to understand it.
– Ms. C 18v (OC, P. 259)

❧

For the grace of God has appeared for the
salvation of all men, training us to renounce
irreligion and worldly passions, and to live
sober, upright, and godly lives in this world.
– TITUS 2:11-12

64.
GOOD WORKS

I do not scorn deep thoughts that nourish the
soul and unite it to God, but long have I known
that we mustn't depend on them and make
perfection consist in receiving lots of light.
The most beautiful thoughts are nothing
without their corresponding works.
– Ms. C 19v (OC, P. 260)

☙

So faith by itself, if it has no works, is dead.
– JAMES 2:17

65.
INSTRUMENTS OF GOD'S WORK

The Lord hasn't changed the way He does
things; He has always used His creatures as
instruments to accomplish His work in souls.
– Ms. C 20R (OC, P. 261)

If any one purifies himself from what is
ignoble, then he will be a vessel for noble use,
consecrated and useful to the master of the
house, ready for any good work.
– 2 TIMOTHY 2:21

66.
KNOWING ONLY JESUS

I can tell I must necessarily forget my own
preferences and personal ideas. I know souls
need to be guided along the path Jesus has
marked out for them, without trying to get
them to walk along my own path.
– Ms. C 22v-23r (OC, P. 265)

৵

For I decided to know nothing among you
except Jesus Christ and him crucified. And I
was with you in weakness and in much fear
and trembling; and my speech and my
message were not in plausible words of
wisdom, but in demonstration of the Spirit
and of power, that your faith might not rest in
the wisdom of men but in the power of God.
– 1 CORINTHIANS 2:2-5

67.
PRAYER AND JOY

For me, prayer is my heart soaring; it is a
simple gaze cast toward Heaven; it is a cry of
gratitude and love in the midst of both trials
and joy; finally, it is something grand that
opens up my soul and unites me to Jesus.
– Ms. C 25R-25V (OC, P. 268)

⁓

Is any one among you suffering? Let him pray.
Is any cheerful? Let him sing praise.
– JAMES 5:13

68.
GOD'S GOODNESS

Ah! The Lord is so good to me, I can't possibly
fear Him; He has always given me what I
longed for, or rather He has always made me
long for what He wanted to give me.
– Ms. C 31R (OC, P. 277)

࿇

"For my yoke is easy, and my burden is light."
– MATTHEW 11:30

69.
GIVING ALL TO GOD

Just as a torrent rushing down into the ocean
carries along everything encountered on the
way, so, O my Jesus, does the soul who plunges
into the bottomless ocean of Your love pull
along with it all the treasures it has.[12]
– Ms. C 34R (OC, P. 281)

And he said, "Truly I tell you, this poor
widow has put in more than all of them;
for they all contributed out of their
abundance, but she out of her poverty
put in all the living that she had."
– LUKE 21:3-4

---

[12] The following sentence in Thérèse's text makes it clear
that those treasures are the souls entrusted to her.

70.
GOD'S OWN LOVE

To love You as You love me, I need to
borrow Your own love; then and only
then do I find rest.
– MS. C 35R (OC, P. 282)

❧

In this the love of God was made manifest
among us, that God sent his only Son into the
world, so that we might live through him.
– 1 JOHN 4:9

71.
LIVING IN HIM

I ask Jesus to pull me into the flames of His
love, to unite me so intimately to Him that
He may live and act through me.
– Ms. C 36R (OC, P. 284)

&

"In him we live and move and have our being."
– ACTS 17:28

72.
IN HIS FOOTSTEPS

Since Jesus has gone back up to Heaven,
I can only follow Him by the footsteps He
has left, but what light His footsteps give off,
how fragrant they are! I need only glance
at the Holy Gospel; as soon as I do, I
breathe in the fragrance of Jesus' life
and I know which way to run.
– Ms. C 36v (OC, pp. 284-285)

For to this you have been called, because
Christ also suffered for you, leaving you an
example, that you should follow in his steps.
– 1 PETER 2:21

73.
CALLED TO LOVE

O Jesus, my Love. I have found my vocation
at last; my vocation is Love!
– Ms. B 3v (OC, P. 226)

෨

And he said to him, "You shall love the Lord
your God with all your heart, and with all your
soul, and with all your mind. This is the great
and first commandment. And a second is like
it, You shall love your neighbor as yourself.
On these two commandments depend
all the law and the prophets."
– MATTHEW 22:37-40

74.
REJOICING AT ALL TIMES

I will sing even when I have to gather my
flowers in the midst of thorns, and my song
will be all the more melodious as the
thorns are long and sharp.
– Ms. B 4v (OC, p. 228)

꙳

Rejoice in the Lord always;
again I will say, Rejoice.
– PHILIPPIANS 4:4

75.
CARRYING THE CROSS

Yes, my heart's dear one, Jesus is here with His cross.[13] Since you are one of His favorites, He wants to make you into His likeness; why be afraid that you will not have the strength to carry this cross without a struggle? On the way to Calvary, Jesus did indeed fall three times and you, poor little child, would like to be different from your spouse, would rather not fall a hundred times if necessary to prove your love to Him by getting back up with even more strength than before your fall!
– LT 81 TO CELINE, JANUARY 1889 (OC, P. 379)

❧

And he said to all, "If any man would come after me, let him deny himself and take up his cross daily and follow me."
– LUKE 9:23

---

[13] This is a reference to their father's illness.

76.
FAITHFULNESS TO
GOD'S COMMANDS

Be faithful to Jesus' words; there you have
the sole condition of our happiness,
the proof of our love for Him.
– LT 165 TO CELINE, JULY 7, 1894 (OC, P. 498)

❧

"If you love me, you will keep my
commandments."
– JOHN 14:15

77.
GOD'S TIMELESSNESS

It seems to me that love can make up for not
having lived a long life. Jesus doesn't pay
attention to time since time no longer exists in
Heaven. He must only pay attention to love.
– LT 114 TO MOTHER AGNES OF JESUS,[14]
SEPTEMBER 3, 1890 (OC, P. 420)

❧

Jesus Christ is the same yesterday
and today and for ever.
– HEBREWS 13:8

---

[14] Thérèse's sister Pauline.

78.
SET YOUR MINDS
ON THINGS ABOVE

Let us lift ourselves above passing things;
let us keep ourselves above the earth; up high
the air is pure; Jesus is hidden, but we
can tell He is there.
– LT 57 TO CELINE, JULY 23, 1888 (OC, P. 350)

৵

Set your minds on things that are above,
not on things that are on earth.
– COLOSSIANS 3:2

79.
WORK MOTIVATED BY LOVE

Love can do anything; the most impossible
things do not seem insurmountable to love.
Jesus does not pay as much attention to the
greatness of our acts, or even to how difficult
they are, as to the love that motivates them.
– LT 65 TO CELINE, OCTOBER 20, 1888
(OC, P. 360)

❧

Whatever your task, work heartily, as serving
the Lord and not men, knowing that from the
Lord you will receive the inheritance as your
reward; you are serving the Lord Christ.
– COLOSSIANS 3:23-24

80.
HUMILITY

If you are willing to bear peacefully the trial of
being dissatisfied with yourself, you will give
me a comfortable safe haven.[15]
– LT 211 TO CELINE (SISTER GENEVIEVE)
DECEMBER 24, 1896 (OC, P. 567)

࿐

He leads the humble in what is right,
and teaches the humble his way.
– PSALM 25:9

---

[15] Signed: Mary, Queen of little angels.

81.
OUR SHARE WITH JESUS

Ah! The truth is that Jesus has such
unfathomable love for us that He wants us to
have a share with Him in saving souls.
He does not want to do anything without us.
– LT 135 TO CELINE, AUGUST 15, 1892
(OC, P. 449)

❧

See what love the Father has given us,
that we should be called children of God;
and so we are.
– 1 JOHN 3:1

82.
BELONGING TO GOD

My Jesus' glory, that is all that matters.
As for mine, I surrender it to Him, and if He
seems to forget me, well, He is free to do so
since I am no longer mine but His.
– LT 103 TO SISTER AGNES OF JESUS,
MAY 4 (?), 1890 (OC, PP. 406-407)

෨

You are not your own;
you were bought with a price.
– 1 CORINTHIANS 6:19-20

83.
GOD SATISFIES

Never does the Good Lord inspire desires
that He cannot fulfill.
– LT 197 TO SISTER MARIE OF THE SACRED
HEART,[16] SEPTEMBER 17, 1896 (OC, P. 553)

৵

"And the LORD will guide you continually,
and satisfy your desire with good things."
– ISAIAH 58:11

---

[16] Thérèse's eldest sister and godmother, Marie.

84.
DRAW NEAR TO GOD

I beg you, do not languish at His feet anymore;
follow your first impulse and throw yourself
into His arms. That is where you belong.
– LT 261 TO FATHER MAURICE BELLIÈRE,
JULY 26, 1897 (OC, P. 619)

❧

Draw near to God and he
will draw near to you.
– JAMES 4:8

85.
SURRENDER

Jesus wants your heart to be totally His.
– LT 244 TO FATHER MAURICE BELLIÈRE,
JUNE 9, 1897 (OC, P. 600)

"So therefore, whoever of you does not
renounce all that he has cannot be my disciple."
– LUKE 14:33

86.
ETERNAL LIFE

Death will not come to get me,
the Good Lord will.
– MAY 1, 1 (OC, P. 995)

❧

For since we believe that Jesus died and rose
again, even so, through Jesus, God will bring
with him those who have fallen asleep.
– 1 THESSALONIANS 4:14

87.
POSITIVE THINKING

I always see the cheerful side of things. Some
people take everything badly, constantly
getting hurt. For me, it's quite the opposite.
– MAY 27, 6 (OC, P. 1004)

Finally, brethren, whatever is true, whatever is
honorable, whatever is just, whatever is pure,
whatever is lovely, whatever is gracious, if
there is any excellence, if there is anything
worthy of praise, think about these things.
– PHILIPPIANS 4:8

88.
LONGING FOR GOOD THINGS

The Good Lord has always made me long
for what He wanted to give me.
– JULY 13, 15 (OC, P. 1041)

❧

No good thing does the LORD withhold
from those who walk uprightly.
– PSALM 84:11

89.
GOD CHOOSES WHOM
HE PLEASES

The Good Lord chooses whomever He
pleases to represent Him.
– JULY 20, 2 (OC, P. 1052)

෨

"The Most High rules the kingdom of men,
and gives it to whom he will."
– DANIEL 4:25

90.
WORRY

As for us who run along the path of Love,
I find we shouldn't think about what painful
things might happen to us in the future, for
that is a lack of trust, and it is as if we were
getting involved in creating.
– JULY 23, 3 (OC, P. 1054)

੭

"Therefore do not be anxious, saying, 'What
shall we eat?' or 'What shall we drink?' or
'What shall we wear?' For the Gentiles seek
all these things; and your heavenly Father
knows that you need them all."
– MATTHEW 6:31-32

91.
CONTINUING AFTER FAILURE

When you accept the embarrassment of having been mean, the Good Lord comes right back.
– SEPTEMBER 2, 6 (OC, P. 1120)

❧

Not that I have already obtained this or am already perfect; but I press on to make it my own, because Christ Jesus has made me his own. Brethren, I do not consider that I have made it my own; but one thing I do, forgetting what lies behind and straining forward to what lies ahead, I press on toward the goal for the prize of the upward call of God in Christ Jesus.
– PHILIPPIANS 3:12-14

92.
LIFE AND ETERNITY

Let us look at life as it truly is:
an instant between two eternities.
– LT 87 TO CELINE, APRIL 4, 1889
(OC, P. 386)

༄

What is your life? For you are a mist that
appears for a little time and then vanishes.
– JAMES 4:14

93.
JESUS CARES

Courage, Jesus hears even the
last echo of our pain.[17]
– LT 85 TO CELINE, MARCH 12, 1889

෨

Cast all your anxieties on him,
for he cares about you.
– 1 PETER 5:7

---

[17] OC, p. 1306, note 4, for LT 85 indicates that this comes
from a letter written by Father Almire Pichon, S.J., to
Sister Marie of the Sacred Heart.

94.
GIVING ONE'S SELF

Loving is surrendering everything,
as well as one's self.
– PRAYER 54, STANZA 22 (OC, P. 755)

❧

By this we know love, that he laid down
his life for us; and we ought to lay down
our lives for the brethren.
– 1 JOHN 3:16

95.
LOVING GOD ABOVE ALL

The one and only good is to love God with your
whole heart and to be poor in spirit here below.
– Ms. A 32v (OC, p. 121)

꙳

And there is nothing upon earth
that I desire besides thee.
My flesh and my heart may fail,
but God is the strength of my heart
and my portion for ever.
– PSALM 73:25-26

96.
GOD'S DIRECTION

More than ever, I understand that the
slightest events of our lives are directed
by God; He is the one who makes us
desire and fulfills all our longing.
– LT 201 TO FATHER ADOLPHE ROULLAND,
NOVEMBER 1, 1896 (OC, PP. 557-558)

❧

"For I know the plans I have for you, says the
LORD, plans for welfare and not for evil, to give
you a future and a hope."
– JEREMIAH 29:11

97.
REDEMPTIVE SUFFERING

When you want to reach a goal, you need to use
the proper means; Jesus made me understand
that He wanted to give me souls through the
cross, and my attraction for suffering grew at
the same pace as my suffering increased.
– Ms. A 69v (OC, p. 187)

⁂

If we are afflicted, it is for your comfort
and salvation; and if we are comforted, it
is for your comfort, which you experience
when you patiently endure the same
sufferings that we suffer.
– 2 CORINTHIANS 1:6

98.
CHRIST ALONE

Now I have no desires anymore, except to
love Jesus to the utmost extreme.
My childish desires have flown away.
– Ms. A 82v (OC, P. 210)

❧

"And there is salvation in no one else, for there
is no other name under heaven given among
men by which we must be saved."
– ACTS 4:12

99.
TREASURE

It is hard to believe how large my heart seems
to me when I take into account all of the earth's
treasures, since I can see that all of them
together could not satisfy it.
– LT 74 TO MOTHER AGNES OF JESUS,
JANUARY 6, 1889 (OC, P. 370)

&

"For where your treasure is, there will
your heart be also."
– MATTHEW 6:21

100.
WHAT IS HIDDEN

For five years, this was my path, but on the outside my suffering could not be seen; it was all the more painful, as I was the only one who knew about it. Oh! How surprised we will be at the end of the world when we read the stories of souls! So many people will be surprised to see the path on which mine was led!
– Ms. A 69V-70R (OC, P. 187)

ॐ

Therefore do not pronounce judgment before the time, before the Lord comes, who will bring to light the things now hidden in darkness and will disclose the purposes of the heart. Then every man will receive his commendation from God.
– 1 CORINTHIANS 4:5